GARDEN PLANNER JOURNAL

SEASONAL TASK

SEASON__________________

GARDEN BEDS/ROW
☐
☐
☐
☐
☐
☐
☐
☐
☐

MAINTENANCE
☐
☐
☐
☐
☐
☐
☐
☐
☐

FERTILIZER
☐
☐
☐
☐
☐
☐
☐
☐
☐

PLANTING/HARVESTING
☐
☐
☐
☐
☐
☐
☐
☐
☐

Seed Inventory

CROP NAME	OTY	SOURCE	PURCHASE DATE	BUY MORE	YEAR
				Y/N	
				Y/N	
				Y/N	
				Y/N	
				Y/N	
				Y/N	
				Y/N	
				Y/N	
				Y/N	
				Y/N	
				Y/N	
				Y/N	
				Y/N	
				Y/N	
				Y/N	
				Y/N	
				Y/N	
				Y/N	
				Y/N	
				Y/N	

Seed Purchase

CROP VARIETY	OTY	COST	SOURCE	DISCOUNT

Monthly Garden Calendar

Month:__________

SUN	MON	TUE	WED	THU	FRD	SAT
☐	☐	☐	☐	☐	☐	☐
☐	☐	☐	☐	☐	☐	☐
☐	☐	☐	☐	☐	☐	☐
☐	☐	☐	☐	☐	☐	☐
☐	☐	☐	☐	☐	☐	☐
☐	☐	☐	☐	☐	☐	☐

Notes

Garden Layout

Garden Layout

Seed Inventory

PLANT NAME	OTY	DESCRIPTION	WHERE TO BUY	WHEN TO BUY	
					☐
					☐
					☐
					☐
					☐
					☐
					☐
					☐
					☐
					☐
					☐
					☐
					☐
					☐
					☐
					☐
					☐
					☐
					☐
					☐

Plant Log

Crop Variety/Plant	Best Season to Plant	Plant Description	Additional Notes

Fertilizer Inventory

FERTILIZER	DESCRIPTION	PLANTS TO APPLY	OTY	BUY MORE	YEAR
				Y/N	
				Y/N	
				Y/N	
				Y/N	
				Y/N	
				Y/N	
				Y/N	
				Y/N	
				Y/N	
				Y/N	
				Y/N	
				Y/N	
				Y/N	
				Y/N	
				Y/N	
				Y/N	
				Y/N	
				Y/N	
				Y/N	
				Y/N	

Gardening Budget

ITEM	AMOUNT	AMOUNT SAVED

ITEM	AMOUNT	AMOUNT SAVED

ITEM	AMOUNT	AMOUNT SAVED

ITEM	AMOUNT	AMOUNT SAVED

Seed Starting Log

Crop/Seds	Date Planted	Date Germinated	Date Transplanted	Additional Notes

Expense Log

DATE	ITEM NAME	DESCRIPTION	OTY	COST	NOTES

PRODUCE BUDGET

FRUIT	VEGETABLES	WEIGHT	OTY	MONTHLY REVENUE	YEARLY REVENUE

Pest Control

Pest	Plants Affected	Bed/Raw	Problem	Tratament	Results

SEASONAL CHECKLIST

SPRING

SUMMER

FALL

WINTER

Monthly Garden Tasks

Top Priorities

To Do List

List of plants to try

Water

Sunlight

Fertilizer

Notes

Monthly Garden Tasks

To Do List

Plant Name ____________________

Crop Variety ____________________

Fertilizer ____________________

Germination Date ____________________

Harvest Date ____________________

Seed Source ____________________

Plating instruction

____

____

____

____

____

____

____

____

____

____

Water

Sunlight

Fertilizer

Notes

____

____

____

Monthly To-Do List

Plant/Crop	Top Priorities	To-Do List

Pest and Disease Control

Pest/ Disease	Plants Affected	Bed/Raw	Problem	Tratament	Results

Monthly Garden Calendar

Month:__________

SUN	MON	TUE	WED	THU	FRD	SAT
☐	☐	☐	☐	☐	☐	☐
☐	☐	☐	☐	☐	☐	☐
☐	☐	☐	☐	☐	☐	☐
☐	☐	☐	☐	☐	☐	☐
☐	☐	☐	☐	☐	☐	☐
☐	☐	☐	☐	☐	☐	☐

Notes

Garden Layout

SEASONAL TASK

SEASON________________

GARDEN BEDS/ROW
☐
☐
☐
☐
☐
☐
☐
☐
☐

MAINTENANCE
☐
☐
☐
☐
☐
☐
☐
☐
☐

FERTILIZER
☐
☐
☐
☐
☐
☐
☐
☐
☐

PLANTING/HARVESTING
☐
☐
☐
☐
☐
☐
☐
☐
☐

Seed Inventory

CROP NAME	OTY	SOURCE	PURCHASE DATE	BUY MORE	YEAR
				Y/N	
				Y/N	
				Y/N	
				Y/N	
				Y/N	
				Y/N	
				Y/N	
				Y/N	
				Y/N	
				Y/N	
				Y/N	
				Y/N	
				Y/N	
				Y/N	
				Y/N	
				Y/N	
				Y/N	
				Y/N	
				Y/N	
				Y/N	

Garden Layout

Seed Purchase

CROP VARIETY	OTY	COST	SOURCE	DISCOUNT

Plant Log

Crop Variety/Plant	Best Season to Plant	Plant Description	Additional Notes

Fertilizer Inventory

FERTILIZER	DESCRIPTION	PLANTS TO APPLY	QTY	BUY MORE	YEAR
				Y/N	
				Y/N	
				Y/N	
				Y/N	
				Y/N	
				Y/N	
				Y/N	
				Y/N	
				Y/N	
				Y/N	
				Y/N	
				Y/N	
				Y/N	
				Y/N	
				Y/N	
				Y/N	
				Y/N	
				Y/N	
				Y/N	
				Y/N	

Seed Inventory

PLANT NAME	OTY	DESCRIPTION	WHERE TO BUY	WHEN TO BUY	
					☐
					☐
					☐
					☐
					☐
					☐
					☐
					☐
					☐
					☐
					☐
					☐
					☐
					☐
					☐
					☐
					☐
					☐
					☐
					☐

Gardening Budget

ITEM	AMOUNT	AMOUNT SAVED

ITEM	AMOUNT	AMOUNT SAVED

ITEM	AMOUNT	AMOUNT SAVED

ITEM	AMOUNT	AMOUNT SAVED

Expense Log

DATE	ITEM NAME	DESCRIPTION	OTY	COST	NOTES

Seed Starting Log

Crop/Seds	Date Planted	Date Germinated	Date Transplanted	Additional Notes

SEASONAL CHECKLIST

SPRING

SUMMER

FALL

WINTER

Pest Control

Pest	Plants Affected	Bed/Raw	Problem	Tratament	Results

PRODUCE BUDGET

FRUIT	VEGETABLES	WEIGHT	OTY	MONTHLY REVENUE	YEARLY REVENUE

Monthly Garden Tasks

Top Priorities

To Do List

List of plants to try

Water

Sunlight

Fertilizer

Notes

Monthly To-Do List

Plant/Crop	Top Priorities	To-Do List

Pest and Disease Control

Pest/ Disease	Plants Affected	Bed/Raw	Problem	Tratament	Results

Monthly Garden Calendar

Month:__________

SUN	MON	TUE	WED	THU	FRD	SAT
☐	☐	☐	☐	☐	☐	☐
☐	☐	☐	☐	☐	☐	☐
☐	☐	☐	☐	☐	☐	☐
☐	☐	☐	☐	☐	☐	☐
☐	☐	☐	☐	☐	☐	☐
☐	☐	☐	☐	☐	☐	☐

Notes

Garden Layout

Garden Layout

SEASONAL TASK

SEASON____________________

GARDEN BEDS/ROW
☐
☐
☐
☐
☐
☐
☐
☐
☐

MAINTENANCE
☐
☐
☐
☐
☐
☐
☐
☐
☐

FERTILIZER
☐
☐
☐
☐
☐
☐
☐
☐
☐

PLANTING/HARVESTING
☐
☐
☐
☐
☐
☐
☐
☐
☐

Seed Inventory

CROP NAME	OTY	SOURCE	PURCHASE DATE	BUY MORE	YEAR
				Y/N	
				Y/N	
				Y/N	
				Y/N	
				Y/N	
				Y/N	
				Y/N	
				Y/N	
				Y/N	
				Y/N	
				Y/N	
				Y/N	
				Y/N	
				Y/N	
				Y/N	
				Y/N	
				Y/N	
				Y/N	
				Y/N	
				Y/N	

Seed Purchase

CROP VARIETY	OTY	COST	SOURCE	DISCOUNT

Seed Inventory

PLANT NAME	OTY	DESCRIPTION	WHERE TO BUY	WHEN TO BUY	
					☐
					☐
					☐
					☐
					☐
					☐
					☐
					☐
					☐
					☐
					☐
					☐
					☐
					☐
					☐
					☐
					☐
					☐
					☐
					☐

Plant Log

Crop Variety/Plant	Best Season to Plant	Plant Description	Additional Notes

Gardening Budget

ITEM	AMOUNT	AMOUNT SAVED

ITEM	AMOUNT	AMOUNT SAVED

ITEM	AMOUNT	AMOUNT SAVED

ITEM	AMOUNT	AMOUNT SAVED

Fertilizer Inventory

FERTILIZER	DESCRIPTION	PLANTS TO APPLY	OTY	BUY MORE	YEAR
				Y/N	
				Y/N	
				Y/N	
				Y/N	
				Y/N	
				Y/N	
				Y/N	
				Y/N	
				Y/N	
				Y/N	
				Y/N	
				Y/N	
				Y/N	
				Y/N	
				Y/N	
				Y/N	
				Y/N	
				Y/N	
				Y/N	
				Y/N	

Expense Log

DATE	ITEM NAME	DESCRIPTION	OTY	COST	NOTES

Seed Starting Log

Crop/Seds	Date Planted	Date Germinated	Date Transplanted	Additional Notes

SEASONAL CHECKLIST

SPRING	SUMMER

FALL	WINTER

Pest Control

Pest	Plants Affected	Bed/Raw	Problem	Tratament	Results

PRODUCE BUDGET

FRUIT	VEGETABLES	WEIGHT	OTY	MONTHLY REVENUE	YEARLY REVENUE

Monthly Garden Tasks

Top Priorities

To Do List

List of plants to try

Water

Sunlight

Fertilizer

Notes

Monthly To-Do List

Plant/Crop	Top Priorities	To-Do List

Pest and Disease Control

Pest/ Disease	Plants Affected	Bed/Raw	Problem	Tratament	Results

Garden Layout

Monthly Garden Calendar

Month:__________

SUN	MON	TUE	WED	THU	FRD	SAT
☐	☐	☐	☐	☐	☐	☐
☐	☐	☐	☐	☐	☐	☐
☐	☐	☐	☐	☐	☐	☐
☐	☐	☐	☐	☐	☐	☐
☐	☐	☐	☐	☐	☐	☐
☐	☐	☐	☐	☐	☐	☐

Notes

Garden Layout

SEASONAL TASK

SEASON____________________

GARDEN BEDS/ROW
☐
☐
☐
☐
☐
☐
☐
☐
☐

MAINTENANCE
☐
☐
☐
☐
☐
☐
☐
☐
☐

FERTILIZER
☐
☐
☐
☐
☐
☐
☐
☐
☐

PLANTING/HARVESTING
☐
☐
☐
☐
☐
☐
☐
☐
☐

Seed Inventory

CROP NAME	OTY	SOURCE	PURCHASE DATE	BUY MORE	YEAR
				Y/N	
				Y/N	
				Y/N	
				Y/N	
				Y/N	
				Y/N	
				Y/N	
				Y/N	
				Y/N	
				Y/N	
				Y/N	
				Y/N	
				Y/N	
				Y/N	
				Y/N	
				Y/N	
				Y/N	
				Y/N	
				Y/N	
				Y/N	

Seed Purchase

CROP VARIETY	OTY	COST	SOURCE	DISCOUNT

Plant Log

Crop Variety/Plant	Best Season to Plant	Plant Description	Additional Notes

Fertilizer Inventory

FERTILIZER	DESCRIPTION	PLANTS TO APPLY	OTY	BUY MORE	YEAR
				Y/N	
				Y/N	
				Y/N	
				Y/N	
				Y/N	
				Y/N	
				Y/N	
				Y/N	
				Y/N	
				Y/N	
				Y/N	
				Y/N	
				Y/N	
				Y/N	
				Y/N	
				Y/N	
				Y/N	
				Y/N	
				Y/N	
				Y/N	

Seed Inventory

PLANT NAME	QTY	DESCRIPTION	WHERE TO BUY	WHEN TO BUY	
					☐
					☐
					☐
					☐
					☐
					☐
					☐
					☐
					☐
					☐
					☐
					☐
					☐
					☐
					☐
					☐
					☐
					☐
					☐
					☐

Gardening Budget

ITEM	AMOUNT	AMOUNT SAVED

ITEM	AMOUNT	AMOUNT SAVED

ITEM	AMOUNT	AMOUNT SAVED

ITEM	AMOUNT	AMOUNT SAVED

Expense Log

DATE	ITEM NAME	DESCRIPTION	OTY	COST	NOTES

Seed Starting Log

Crop/Seds	Date Planted	Date Germinated	Date Transplanted	Additional Notes

PRODUCE BUDGET

FRUIT	VEGETABLES	WEIGHT	OTY	MONTHLY REVENUE	YEARLY REVENUE

Pest Control

Pest	Plants Affected	Bed/Raw	Problem	Tratament	Results

SEASONAL CHECKLIST

SPRING

SUMMER

FALL

WINTER

Monthly Garden Tasks

Top Priorities

To Do List

List of plants to try

Water

Sunlight

Fertilizer

Notes

Monthly To-Do List

Plant/Crop	Top Priorities	To-Do List

Pest and Disease Control

Pest/ Disease	Plants Affected	Bed/Raw	Problem	Tratament	Results

Monthly Garden Calendar

*Month:*____________

SUN	MON	TUE	WED	THU	FRD	SAT
☐	☐	☐	☐	☐	☐	☐
☐	☐	☐	☐	☐	☐	☐
☐	☐	☐	☐	☐	☐	☐
☐	☐	☐	☐	☐	☐	☐
☐	☐	☐	☐	☐	☐	☐
☐	☐	☐	☐	☐	☐	☐

Notes

Garden Layout

Garden Layout

SEASONAL TASK

SEASON____________________

GARDEN BEDS/ROW
☐
☐
☐
☐
☐
☐
☐
☐
☐

MAINTENANCE
☐
☐
☐
☐
☐
☐
☐
☐
☐

FERTILIZER
☐
☐
☐
☐
☐
☐
☐
☐
☐

PLANTING/HARVESTING
☐
☐
☐
☐
☐
☐
☐
☐
☐

Seed Purchase

CROP VARIETY	OTY	COST	SOURCE	DISCOUNT

Seed Inventory

CROP NAME	OTY	SOURCE	PURCHASE DATE	BUY MORE	YEAR
				Y/N	
				Y/N	
				Y/N	
				Y/N	
				Y/N	
				Y/N	
				Y/N	
				Y/N	
				Y/N	
				Y/N	
				Y/N	
				Y/N	
				Y/N	
				Y/N	
				Y/N	
				Y/N	
				Y/N	
				Y/N	
				Y/N	
				Y/N	

Plant Log

Crop Variety/Plant	Best Season to Plant	Plant Description	Additional Notes

Seed Inventory

PLANT NAME	OTY	DESCRIPTION	WHERE TO BUY	WHEN TO BUY	
					☐
					☐
					☐
					☐
					☐
					☐
					☐
					☐
					☐
					☐
					☐
					☐
					☐
					☐
					☐
					☐
					☐
					☐
					☐
					☐

Fertilizer Inventory

FERTILIZER	DESCRIPTION	PLANTS TO APPLY	QTY	BUY MORE	YEAR
				Y/N	
				Y/N	
				Y/N	
				Y/N	
				Y/N	
				Y/N	
				Y/N	
				Y/N	
				Y/N	
				Y/N	
				Y/N	
				Y/N	
				Y/N	
				Y/N	
				Y/N	
				Y/N	
				Y/N	
				Y/N	
				Y/N	
				Y/N	

Gardening Budget

ITEM	AMOUNT	AMOUNT SAVED

ITEM	AMOUNT	AMOUNT SAVED

ITEM	AMOUNT	AMOUNT SAVED

ITEM	AMOUNT	AMOUNT SAVED

Seed Starting Log

Crop/Seds	Date Planted	Date Germinated	Date Transplanted	Additional Notes

Expense Log

DATE	ITEM NAME	DESCRIPTION	OTY	COST	NOTES

PRODUCE BUDGET

FRUIT	VEGETABLES	WEIGHT	OTY	MONTHLY REVENUE	YEARLY REVENUE

SEASONAL CHECKLIST

SPRING

SUMMER

FALL

WINTER

Pest Control

Pest	Plants Affected	Bed/Raw	Problem	Tratament	Results

Pest and Disease Control

Pest/ Disease	Plants Affected	Bed/Raw	Problem	Tratament	Results

Monthly Garden Tasks

Top Priorities

To Do List

List of plants to try

Water

Sunlight

Fertilizer

Notes

Monthly To-Do List

Plant/Crop	Top Priorities	To-Do List

Monthly Garden Calendar

Month:__________

SUN	MON	TUE	WED	THU	FRD	SAT
☐	☐	☐	☐	☐	☐	☐
☐	☐	☐	☐	☐	☐	☐
☐	☐	☐	☐	☐	☐	☐
☐	☐	☐	☐	☐	☐	☐
☐	☐	☐	☐	☐	☐	☐
☐	☐	☐	☐	☐	☐	☐

Notes

Garden Layout

Notes

Thank you!

WE ARE GLAD THAT YOU PURCHASED OUR BOOK!
PLEASE LET US KNOW HOW WE CAN IMPROVE IT!
YOUR FEEDBACK IS ESSENTIAL TO US.

Contact us at:

log'Sin@gmail.com

JUST TITLE THE EMAIL 'CREATIVE' AND WE WILL GIVE YOU SOME EXTRA SURPRISES!

Thank you!

WE ARE GLAD THAT YOU PURCHASED OUR BOOK!
PLEASE LET US KNOW HOW WE CAN IMPROVE IT!
YOUR FEEDBACK IS ESSENTIAL TO US.

Contact us at:

log'Sin@gmail.com

JUST TITLE THE EMAIL 'CREATIVE' AND WE WILL GIVE YOU SOME EXTRA SURPRISES!

CPSIA information can be obtained
at www.ICGtesting.com
Printed in the USA
LVHW061449221222
735718LV00013B/502

9 781803 851952